Starting a Community Choir

Using Music in Outreach and Mission

Ordaine fficer

GROVE BOOKS LIMITED
RIDLEY HALL RD CAMBRIDGE CB3 9HU

Contents

Church Mission Society supports the Grove Mission and Evangelism Series
At Church Mission Society, we believe that every Christian is called to join in God's mission, whether that means crossing the street or crossing continents, and we want to set people free to put that call into action.

Acknowledgments
A huge thank you to the choirs I have had the joy to work with. In particular, thank you to those mentioned in this booklet: Cum Vino Cantus, St Michael's Teen Worship Band, Belsize Community Choir, Chapelfields Community Choir, and the University of Coventry Student and Staff Choir.

First Impression August 2022
ISSN 2399-6536
ISBN 978 1 78827 257 5

1

Introduction

> I will sing to the Lord as long as I live; I will sing praise to my God while I have being.
>
> Ps 104.33

Throughout our ecclesial history, the church has used the potential of music and art to be propositional, conveying both theological and devotional meaning. Singing sacred music (I include both traditional and contemporary worship) allows people to connect with God while they explore their spiritual questions in a non-threatening environment. Music and pictorial arts have always had some place within the church, for not only spiritual and didactic purposes but, I would also argue, as a type of *midrash*, a 'thinking out loud.'[1]

The intent of this booklet is to focus on the evangelistic aspects of building community choirs and the benefit of using choral music gently to bring people to Christ.

It was written with three groups in mind: church leaders who make the decisions and could facilitate the project happening; choir leaders or people with musical skills interested in taking the lead; and perhaps a choir member who is not in leadership but would want to encourage and participate in such a project. I expect there is something for each of those groups in what follows.

While there are many resources for music educators and conductors, I have not been able to find any books which include both an outreach or missional rationale for community choirs as well as very basic musical and organizational steps to take. Hopefully, this booklet will start to address that gap.

Reasons Why You Should Start a Community Choir

- Many church communities already have the skill set needed to start a community choir. There is likely a musical director/music minister/worship leader/organist who could easily lead such an activity. As soon as key stakeholders from the church leadership are on board, it takes very little time to organize and advertise.
- There is very little financial cost to the church (we regularly only purchased a few pieces of music a year and either used public

domain or borrowed the rest). Likewise, there is no special equipment the member needs to purchase before joining. Anyone of any age can get involved, regardless of background or experience.

- A choir is one of many potential ministries from an outward-facing church that establishes the church as the centre of the community, helping people associate the name of the church with important community organizations.
- A community choir increases the level of comfort in a church building itself, giving people the opportunity to feel at home in your church. Several members of the community choirs I have worked with did not follow any faith, some had previously been hurt by the church and some were quite militantly atheist. Making them feel at home in a place of worship and having them invite friends to that space was a major step.
- Historically, singing was an important way to mark significant life events with no distinction between the performer and the audience. At a time when many people are reluctant to enter church buildings, they have lost not only the spiritual and communal aspects of a church family—they have also lost the joys and benefits of communal singing.
- A choir is quite easy to adapt and replicate in different settings. I have had the pleasure of starting a community choir from scratch on five occasions in very different contexts (Knox Presbyterian, Calgary, Canada; St Michael's Community, Calgary, Canada; Belsize Park, London; Chapelfields, Coventry; University of Coventry, Coventry) and have been able to build and nurture a community that was a supportive and loving family in each case while performing music at a very high level.
- There are multiple benefits from singing for individual members that include physical, cognitive and emotional health. Other benefits include improved breathing; improved speech and posture; reduced pain levels while singing; improved cognitive functioning; reduced stress; and an increased sense of confidence and well-being.
- A community choir also helps people individually in terms of physical and mental health, reducing social isolation and increasing social networks and involvement in the community. It forms a new family / small group that not only supports each other but that has the potential for a focus of social action and civic engagement through the local charities it supports.

- We recognize the loneliness and social isolation many people experienced during COVID-19 lockdowns while they tried to avoid unnecessary social contact. As we are (hopefully) entering a post-COVID-19 world, a community choir is an excellent vehicle to help people reconnect with wider society beyond their support bubbles.

Start With the Explicit Goal of Creating Community

Most choirs are formed with the explicit intent of meeting musical goals. I have been blessed to conduct a number of those ensembles when I worked as a freelance musician in Canada and in the UK. While important, the goal is clearly different when forming a community choir with the goal of outreach to the wider parish. Music is a vehicle through which we are deliberately able to create community for a lot of people living in social isolation. We provide a place for a new and broader network of relationships that cross class and ethnicity.

If you choose to structure your choir with the specific intent of supporting charities (like two of the community choirs I have worked with did), there is a lot of opportunity for giving back and building connections with the wider parish. There is the potential to increase awareness and support of both local and international charitable organizations such as Christian Aid or Samaritans or Toilet Twinning. This means not only money, but also people being introduced to the specific charity and volunteering time/skills to support that organization as well.

There is also the opportunity to connect with other choral or musical ensembles in your area. By consciously choosing always to invite other performers to share in our concerts, we were reaching out into the wider community and building relationships with other musical organizations as well.

By providing a safe place and a family for members of the community in the choir, the choir can often function in a manner similar (in many, but not all ways) to how effective small groups or cell groups operate. The community choir is a place where the members feel safe, can explore questions, update each other on important aspects of their lives, are supported, are cared for and are prayed for (after permission is received to do so). The group reduces social isolation and increases concern for the wider neighbourhood.

Lastly, language learning—in the last choir I worked with in Coventry, four members of the choir were not originally from the UK. One gentleman of Polish background had quite poor English. One of his stated goals when he joined was to practise speaking and singing English.

> I would argue there are clear indicators suggesting use of music and song in the language-learning environment is both supported theoretically by practising teachers and grounded in the empirical literature as a benefit to increase linguistic, sociocultural and communicative competencies. From an educational standpoint, music and language not only can, but should be studied together.[2]

Your choir could give language learners the opportunity to do so.

Our Journey of Gentle Evangelism through the Community Choir

We redefined (to a certain extent) success and what evangelism meant to us. Was it only more numbers at services? Increased giving? Were we only counting baptisms? (Not saying there is anything wrong with any of those as measures along with other factors, by the way). We looked at what it meant for us to be an outward-facing church and used the community choir to be one of the ministries that helped our local church continue the transition from being inward focused (just keeping things ticking over), to being outward and mission focused. We continued to look outwards towards the communities in our parish (and beyond) that we loved and served by planting seeds and gradually loving people into the kingdom of God, trusting that growth would occur in God's time (1 Cor 3.5–7).

One approach became speaking about our faith (no matter what the response), using the music to introduce topics of discussion informally over a cuppa at the break or more formally in front of the ensemble. We planted seeds and provided a warm supportive environment for them to grow in.

It has been said that it takes many significant encounters to come to faith (however one might understand that phrase). We actively wanted to provide opportunities for those significant encounters in our community choir. The fact that we were starting with music, with story, instead of doctrine or telling them why they are wrong about their life seemed to increase the openness to listen.

Christianity offers a different approach to understanding the world, one that music can and does participate in from an emotional, imaginative perspective. Milbank argues that apologists do not just want to convince people in a rational manner, as if picking up some obscure fact about rainfall in Derby last year: we want a theological approach to apologetics that helps them grasp Christianity in 'a *participatory* way.'[3] Music can help people recognize the 'homesickness' they feel, the longing and searching for the transcendent God—as well as be able to see people, events and the natural world around them as gifts; 'they are recognized as possessing a depth that gestures to God.'[4]

We became increasingly aware of the importance of adaptation and contextualization—about how we shared God's love with others. This is not about moving away from the unchanging message of the love and grace of God (see Heb 13.8–9a), but rather about how we communicate and celebrate that message—'to proclaim afresh in each generation.'

Please also note this was never intended to be underhanded or manipulative. The equivalent of 'You can only sing in the choir when you view the advert for the Church of England. With exegesis, you get a free egg roll!'

Whenever we communicated, we tried to do so in ways that helped others to understand us. This is not a new thing or something watering down the faith. Paul knew the value of ensuring that he identified with his context when speaking about the gospel (1 Cor 9.19–22). Our community choir gave us the opportunity to do the same.

2 Biblical and Theological Reflection

> '...I will extol you, O Lord, among the nations, and sing praises to your name.'
>
> 2 Samuel 22 and Ps 18.49

Music has been a medium for communicating the word since the beginning. Rahner asserts that music and the arts themselves are a form of theology, that by singing or listening to music, a person engages with the love of God:

> One could take the position that what comes to expression in a Rembrandt painting or Bruckner symphony is so inspired and borne by divine revelation, by grace and by God's self-communication, that they communicate something about what the human reality is in the eyes of God which cannot be completely translated into verbal theology...why should a person not think that when he [sic] hears a Bach oratorio, he comes into contact in a very unique way with God's revelation about the human not only by the words it employs, but by the music itself? Why should he not think that what is going on there is theology?[5]

But what does the Bible say about music and singing? While we do not have the space for an exhaustive list, we now briefly turn to the Scriptures. Perhaps David, 'a man after God's own heart' (1 Sam 13.14 and Acts 13.22), might be a good example for us to follow (at least in this area—maybe avoid some other things he did). As someone who was often singing—even when hiding from Saul in a cave (Psalm 57)—and regardless of how you understand the psalms were written—as someone to whom at least half the psalms are attributed, he has much to teach us about singing as prayer and praise. We will touch on both, along with a brief comment on the historic use of music in helping people grapple with the Scriptures as a form of *midrash* to close this chapter.

Singing as Prayer

The phrase, 'One who sings, prays twice,' attributed to Augustine, points to the fact that Christians have been using music in prayer and as part of their corporate encounter with God for centuries. 'Like posture and gesture, singing has been seen not as a decoration or an add-on to the "real prayer" (supposedly delivered into spoken words) but is something which can be prayer in itself.'[6]

There are numerous examples in the Bible of music as prayer and part of worship. We could look at the conclusion of the institution of holy communion in Matthew, for example. Just before the disciples followed Jesus to the Garden of Gethsemane, they worshipped God through music.

> When they had sung the hymn, they went out to the Mount of Olives.
> Matt 26.30

Or in Acts, we see Paul and Silas singing and praying while they were locked in the prison.

> About midnight Paul and Silas were praying and singing hymns to God, and the prisoners were listening to them. Suddenly there was an earthquake, so violent that the foundations of the prison were shaken; and immediately all the doors were opened and everyone's chains were unfastened. (Acts 16.25–26)

In each case, music is used to express something that cannot be said with words alone. Perhaps that is why the important moments in opera and musicals are always sung, just as they often are in church services (regardless of tradition).

Martin Luther once stated that, 'Next to the Word of God, music deserves the highest praise.'[7] You have probably had the experience of leaving a service having a hard time remembering what the main points of the sermon were, but of having a worship song or hymn stuck in your head for the rest of the week (what linguistics calls the 'involuntary mental rehearsal'). But music does not only help us remember scriptural or doctrinal truths. And it does not matter if the new worship song or the choral motet is easy or challenging musically. 'Ordinary churchgoers in Leipzig would listen to Bach cantatas in church. Even if they did not understand the supreme quality and depth to the music, they could enjoy it. The music was not written for an elite.'[8]

Music and singing can be truth bearing and can express concepts words cannot. Perhaps that was also what was happening in the following passage from the Book of Revelation:

> When he had taken the scroll, the four living creatures and the twenty-four elders fell before the Lamb, each holding a harp and golden bowls full of incense, which are the prayers of the saints. They sing a new song:
>
> 'You are worthy to take the scroll and to open its seals, for you were slaughtered and by your blood you ransomed for God saints from every tribe and language and people and nation.' (Rev 5.8–9)

Singing as Praise

> Are any among you suffering? They should pray. Are any cheerful? They should sing songs of praise. (Jas 5.13)

This passage from the Letter to James is a perfect transition from discussing singing as prayer to exploring singing as praise. When words alone do not seem enough, we turn to music. However, I recognize we are caught between the two modes. The music as we sing songs of praise contains more than we can articulate cognitively and critically, but we are all aware of its power. Throughout the Bible, music is used as an expression of praise. There are numerous examples in the psalms, such as Ps 95.1–2; Ps 104.33; or Ps 146.2.

> O come, let us sing to the Lord…let us make a joyful noise to him with songs of praise! (Ps 95.1–2)

This command to praise is not simply something we should do (although that is valid in itself), but also a gift of the heart that we offer to God. It changes us at our core, reminds us of everything in our lives that we are grateful for and leads us to share that love of God with others around us, to declare his glory among the nations.

> Sing to the Lord, all the earth. Tell of his salvation from day to day. Declare his glory among the nations, his marvellous works among all the peoples. For great is the Lord, and greatly to be praised; he is to be revered above all gods. (1 Chron 16.23–25)

Music as a Vehicle to Learn or Grapple with Scripture

Throughout our history, the church has used the potential of music to be propositional, conveying theological and devotional meaning that 'transcends logically contestable truths…less of a logical idea than an imaginative apprehension of truth.'[9] The Scriptures were interpreted by Christian music and art, 'using methods comparable to the verbal form of exegesis.'[10] The Arras Synod (1005) would even declare that 'art teaches the unsettled what they cannot learn from books.'[11]

Just one modern example might be the beautiful Christmas song '*Mary, did you know?*' Many people attending church, for better or for worse, have built a substantial part of their understanding of Mary and the virgin birth on the theology espoused by that piece of music rather than the Magnificat (or 'Mary's Song') found in the Gospel of Luke 1.46–55. Christian music has had an immeasurable impact on the understanding of Scripture and faith of the church.

3 Practical First Steps

> ...as you sing psalms and hymns and spiritual songs among yourselves, singing and making melody to the Lord in your hearts. (Eph 5.19)

Okay, so you are interested in trying to start a choir in your community. What are the first steps? In the same way that I believe anyone can sing, I am certain that it will be possible for you to start a choir as outreach from your church.

In this chapter, I will share some suggestions on how to approach behind-the-scenes administration as you set up and run a choir. Please note that I can only share from my point of view and experience (as a freelance musician, as an educator and as a priest). My thoughts and experience represent my theological, philosophical, pedagogical and musical aesthetic biases. Those biases—those pedagogical and theological underpinnings—may not be appropriate for who you are, for where you sit theologically, or for your context. Of course, please feel free to adapt to your context as much as appropriate or feel free to ignore completely.

Here is what I am going to touch on so we can start thinking about:

- Recruiting
- Setting mission and values
- Accompanist
- Admin support
- Good rehearsal spaces
- Subscriptions
- Organizing rehearsals
- Importance of social time to build community
- Concert flow and planning
- Regularly including prayer

Recruiting

I recommend using social media (whatever platform is popular at the time) and building a basic website. However, in most of the choirs that I was a part of starting from scratch, the old-school approach of word of mouth and putting up posters in the church, schools, colleges, libraries, community centres, local cafes and shops brought in the most people.

The first rehearsal was always a little scary because you had no idea if you would be standing there by yourself or if there would be dozens of people. In all cases, in dramatically different contexts, we had between 14–19 people show up for the first rehearsal.

After that, while we kept advertising with posters or in local newsletters and on social media, the biggest area of growth always occurred because of members bringing friends or because someone saw us in a service or concert, recognized the sense of community and fun (along with singing well) and wanted to be a part of the choir.

An example text you could use:

> Interested in singing? Passionate about choral music performed well? Want to make some new friends in the community? Come join the newly formed non-auditioned _______ Choir!
>
> We are an inclusive, fun, and engaging community that values the playful and relaxed pursuit of choral excellence.
>
> Rehearsals ____ evenings from 7.00–9.00pm @ St ____ Church, _____. (First rehearsal ___). More info: _____

Setting Mission and Values

The first community choir I was blessed to start with some good friends in Calgary, Canada started with no name and eventually evolved both a name (*Cum Vino Cantus*—loosely translated as 'with wine comes singing') and a set of values. The other teen worship band (more about that later) and the three choirs that I started in London and in Coventry were explicitly based on a set of values with a clear mission statement.

As with any organization or business, having a decent mission or vision statement made our direction clearer when making decisions—but also helped people decide if our choir was the right place for them.

An example Mission Statement to use as a starting point:

> The ____ Community Choir first and foremost values the playful and relaxed pursuit of choral excellence. We are an inclusive, fun and engaging community.

Example values/principles to use as a starting point:

- We are a non-auditioned choir who are passionate about choral music.
- We create an environment that is respectful, inclusive and supportive.
- We embrace a blend of eclectic music from secular and sacred traditions worldwide that captures a broad spectrum of human emotion and experience.
- We are an affordable and accessible group that strives to maintain a relaxed, casual and supportive rehearsal and performance atmosphere.
- We are eager to excel as a choral ensemble and value the dedication of our members—welcoming those without choral experience as well as strong experienced singers.
- We value the opportunity to improve musically both as individuals and as a community—and share a desire to expand our understanding of choral music.

Accompanist

If you are not a solid keyboardist / pianist / organist yourself (and even if you are), getting a good accompanist is strongly recommended. It allows the leader some freedom to move around and listen to what is happening in each section, and provides an extra musical ear to help correct pitch / rhythm issues while learning the music.

Administrative Support

As in any ministry, remember to build a team around you. Ideally, aim for a team or committee to assist with decision making (perhaps even repertoire choices), finances, to coordinate performances, to design graphics for concert posters, to help advertise, to work with social media and to plan for drink/ food at the concerts etc. Besides being infinitely more enjoyable with a team around you and less work for you, there is a much stronger chance of sustainability if / when you move on.

Subscriptions

One of the benefits of running the choir as a ministry out of your church building or community hall is that it allows costs to be negligible or non-existent for the choir members. At the very least, rent and insurance could be covered (if not costs associated with the music director and accompanist) within the regular church ministry budget. Additionally, many churches have libraries of choral music (whether there is still a choir functioning there any more or not). It is also easy to borrow original copies from other churches or organizations.

At this point, I need to clearly state, 'Please do not photocopy music.' Besides being illegal and unethical, it deprives composers of their fees and therefore reduces the time they can spend on writing new music. Check out the UK Intellectual Property Office website for more information about copyright and printed music. Please help churches model good ethical behaviour.

Good Rehearsal Spaces

Besides the normal considerations of size of room, how safe the space is, how much it would cost to heat, available parking, how close it is to a kitchen space for tea (and biscuits, wine, cake etc), there are a couple of other things to consider.

First, what are the acoustics of the rehearsal space? It might be best to rehearse in the worship space, but if it is a huge room that is impossible to heat and/ or has been refurbished with a focus on amplified music, it may not be the best place for choral rehearsals. If it is impossible to rehearse in the sanctuary or nave of the church itself, try to find a place with very little carpet or heavy curtains over the windows or fabric on chairs that would absorb sound and dampen the resonance. Choosing a space with a lot of resonance builds confidence quickly in the choir, like a place with hard wood, glass or stone walls. (Of course, before any performance, make sure the choir has a chance to sing in the space the service or concert will take place to get used to the acoustic as well.)

Secondly, how do you wish to set up the seating? There needs to be space to stand as well as to sit when singing. Consider also whether you want the choir set in rows with you at the front, in a more collegiate or cathedral style facing each other, or the set up I often preferred—which was to stand in a circle facing inwards. Rehearsing in a circle allows the singers to see and hear each other easily, to be able to notice visually (as well as aurally) how the different musical phrases fit together, reinforces a sense of equality, and the conductor can easily get close to the different sections or individual singers to hear what is going on. (Of course, as above, make sure the choir has a chance to stand in the formation they will be singing in during the concert or service to get used to hearing different things.)

Organizing Rehearsals

All the choirs I have been blessed to be a part of have had the habit of sharing wine as well as tea and coffee at the break (except for the teen group, obviously). In my opinion, this led to a more relaxed and friendly atmosphere throughout the evening. We would each bring a bottle every now and then and always had enough to share.

Some things to try might be:

- Listing on a white board both the order of the pieces being rehearsed that night and when the break is planned (so music can be put in the right order before rehearsal starts and people know the direction of the rehearsal).
- Keep each section of the rehearsal to 15–20 minutes before a change occurs to keep people interested.
- Always include a short warm up (more about that in the next chapter). This may also be the place for a moment of silence or a short prayer to recentre people from the busyness of the day and help them focus on being present for the rehearsal.
- If there is more than one piano and room in the space, consider splitting so that the accompanist (or musically-skilled choir member) could take one section and you take the other, greatly decreasing the amount of time that people sit while other sections learn their parts.
- Additionally, to reduce individual learning time during rehearsal, I would recommend recording each part on its own, modelling proper pronunciation and where you plan to breathe during the phrase. Then share those files with everyone so that people can listen and practise at home or in the car.
- After a warm up, plan to do a piece that is easily within the choir's comfort zone and does not have extreme volume or range issues. This allows the singers to continue warming up while that piece is being rehearsed (so as not to damage their vocal cords) and builds confidence for the upcoming rehearsal.
- I would then recommend rehearsing the most challenging piece in your repertoire while there is still attention and focus, finding a good place to end before the break so it concludes on a positive note.

- I recommend always ending the rehearsal with either (a) running through a section of something just learned to reinforce that learning; and/or (b) something that is within the choir's comfort zone (perhaps something that is more playful and fun) that they sound good on to end the night with everyone going away feeling positive.

Importance of Social Time to Build Community

Depending on your context and goals, reducing social isolation and building community will likely be a focus of the choir. Some suggestions to try might be:

- Take a 15–20 minute break about half-way through the rehearsal.
- Deliberately start to meet 15 minutes early before the official rehearsal bit begins so that people can talk and catch up.
- Take mini-breaks during rehearsal to encourage members to go and talk to someone they do not know for two or three minutes.
- Encourage them to share aspects of their lives (start each rehearsal with any big news—surprisingly, there is nearly always something, from a new job to graduating to buying a flat to a new grandchild).
- Encourage people to go for a drink after rehearsal.
- Plan events such as bring and share, a Christmas or year-end party.
- 'Carols in the Pub' (or 'Hymns in the Pub').
- Plan performances to have social time afterwards. For example, sing carols for a charity in the market/outside a shop and then all go for mulled wine at someone's house or the local pub.

Concert Flow and Planning

The choir in London and one of the choirs in Coventry that I led both usually planned four major concerts a year (one being leading the carol service at the church). I would also often suggest to the choir that they sing in church before the concert to (a) thank the church for their support; (b) perform the piece more than once; (c) encourage congregation members to attend the concert; (d) help the choir members feel comfortable and welcome in a service.

I have kept with the pattern of sharing a full concert with one or more other choirs, keeping it fairly short to about an hour in total—often without an interval (I would personally much rather hear a choir do 15 minutes of music well than 30 minutes of rubbish)—and it guaranteed an audience of some type (even if it was only the other choir and their family members).

In both Coventry and London, we would also use the concerts to raise money for a local charity. We would invite someone from the charity to talk at the beginning of the concert and to set something up in the hall / gathering area. We made it clear that it was free admission for all with the opportunity to donate before and after at the door to the charity. The fact that we were building relationships with other local choirs and charities often got us more publicity leading up to and after the performances.

I would recommend starting the concert with your choir (so they can be warmed up properly, not sit too long between warm up and performance, and not have time to get freaked out while the other choir(s) sings). This also allows them to relax and focus on hosting the guest ensembles after they perform.

I try to structure the set to open with a strong, comfortable piece (hopefully something upbeat), put slower repertoire and more difficult repertoire in the middle and end with something lively. Try to take the audience / congregation on a short journey throughout your set.

Lastly, I would strongly recommend finding one or two pieces that everyone sings together at the end as a joint choir. This not only ends the concert on a high note (so to speak), but it is always fun for the choirs to sing with a much larger group and it encourages everyone to stay throughout the concert because they are in the last piece. I have found easy-ish pieces like the first movement from Vivaldi's *Gloria* or Mozart's *Ave Verum Corpus* or a four-part setting of *Siyahamba* effective. I have sometimes also asked everyone (audience and choirs) to sing some pieces like *Jerusalem* or *God Save the King* together to close the concert.

Regularly Including Prayer

As expressed earlier, the goal of the groups I worked with was a gentle evangelism. Creating community and well-being was integral. We had members from within the congregation, from other churches in the area, people of other faiths and people of no faith.

That said, it was not unusual to say a prayer at the start of a concert in the church or to pray with people individually at rehearsals who asked for prayer. I often had a large candle lit near the front of the room with a topical printed prayer beside it (for example: for refugees, or for flooding in parts of the country, for Syria or Ukraine). Prayer was available if asked for, and the prayer tree in the gathering area of one of the churches was used quite often by members of the choir.

There were, of course, opportunities to pray in front of the entire choir before or during rehearsals—especially in response to world events or people's lives. I chose to do that rarely to keep everyone included.

4

Musical First Steps

> Can [music] perhaps be a kind of icon, transparent to its eternal ground? Can it perhaps stop us in our tracks and make us aware of a Presence before which we may be transformed?[12]

There are, of course, a variety of excellent texts about the musical and conducting skills required to lead a choir well. I am not going to duplicate those in this short chapter, but we will attempt to explore a couple of ideas that might be helpful. There are many resources that could be recommended, but I would strongly endorse the Royal School of Church Music (RSCM) *Voice for Life* singer's workbooks that teach reading music notation, proper posture for singing and how to breathe well when singing (among many other things).

The following topics will be explored in this chapter, starting from the assumption of a non-auditioned choir that includes a range of experience, natural talent and skill:

- Learning by ear
- Reading music
- Rehearsal suggestions
- Warm ups
- Choosing repertoire
- The first rehearsal
- Lead-up to performances

Learning by Ear

One of the first decisions you might want to make is whether to teach the music completely by ear/by rote or whether to use printed sheet music with the choir. There are many benefits to learning by ear and memorizing the music, including usually knowing the music with more depth, being able to perform some of the stylistic nuances in a way that cannot show up on written music and watching the conductor more during performances. It also clearly allows people to be included who do not read music when they join. It is not, in any way, a lesser choice. There are many cultures and genres historically (and presently) that teach music only by ear. However, it has the downfall of a lot of people waiting while one group learns one part—and often having to repeat teaching from the beginning because there is not a reliable way to notate what was learned.

As a simple approach in a rehearsal, I would sing a short phrase (or ask someone else to model it instead) while a piano played the same line and then ask the choir / section to sing that phrase back to me. I would also move my hand up and down to indicate if the note was going higher or lower in the melody or move it horizontally to indicate a longer note.

Reading Music

That said, I nearly always used music and taught how to read the notation as we learned the music itself in context. For me, it allowed us to learn music together as a group. Like any language, it takes time and happens in small steps. There is a well-accepted hierarchy that many follow in terms of reading music:

- Start with the rhythm
- Add time signatures
- Add clefs and intervals
- Add scales
- Add chords and harmony

Teaching Rhythm

I would always initially introduce reading of rhythm using North American terminology because it shows the mathematical relation between notes and then later transition to British terminology for notation. It is easy for any age group to draw (and understand) how an orange or a cake can be broken down into different sections.

(For example: One Whole note → Two Half notes → Four Quarter notes →Eight Eighth notes…and then also use British names for the notes)

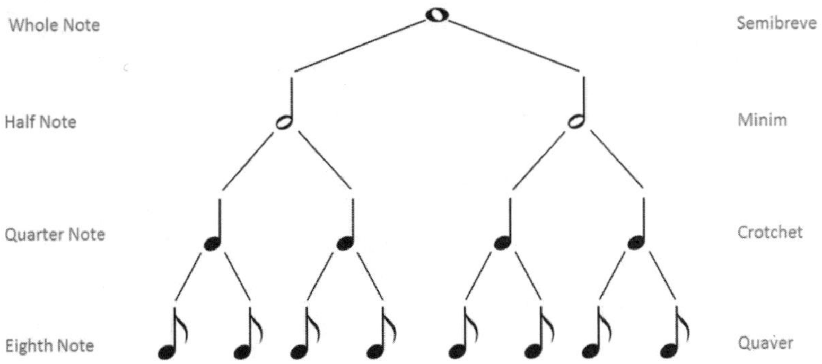

Rehearsal Suggestions

If there are problems while learning something new while reading music, remove either the words and just teach (1) the rhythm—either by clapping it, or asking the choir to tap it on their legs, or sing it on one pitch; (2) then introduce the melody without words and sing to 'la' or 'ta' (depending on whether it was a smooth or more rhythmic musical phrase); (3) then gradually add the words back in. Or you might try just speaking the words in rhythm without any melody and later adding the melody back in.

Warm Ups

There are a variety of ways to do warm ups. Most importantly, it is a time to warm up the voice so the singer does not damage anything, and to get people mentally focused in the room. Some suggestions might be:

- Start with humming up and down the first five notes of the scale ('1,2,3,4,5,4,3,2,1' or 'do, re, mi, fa, so, fa, mi, re, do'), then move to an open 'ah' or 'mah' sound.
- Move through the vowels from back of your mouth to the front—'mah, may, me, mow, moo,' being careful to keep pure vowel sounds on each vowel and not allow diphthongs to occur.[13]
- Start the vocal warm-up in the comfortable lower range and move up by semitone after each phrase. Then return to the same note and move down, slowly, with relaxed open throats. We do not want anyone to force anything too high or too low, as that could potentially damage the vocal cords.
- Take time to relax, stretch, rub shoulders, practise good posture.
- Take time to sit in silence or a gentle guided exercise to reduce stress and increase focus.
- Introduce solfa or solfége and split the group into two sections, each singing different notes following a different hand.[14] Listen to the tuning as each group moves from note to note and different intervals/harmonies occur.
- Practise breathing and proper breath control (for example—breathe in for four, hold for four, release for four on a hissing sound with variations to increase the amount of air people use).
- Practise using your diaphragm to breathe. If choir members are able to lie down and sit back up again, ask them to lie on the floor or a pew/bench and place their hands on their stomachs. It is practically

impossible to breathe shallowly from only your lungs when lying down. This breathing from the diaphragm with the stomach rising and falling each time is what proper breath should look like / feel like when singing.

- Use the warm up to introduce new rhythms or musical concepts.

Choosing Repertoire

As with any of my suggestions, there are multiple ways to approach choosing repertoire. Whatever criteria you use to choose music, keep in mind a balance of the entertainment / engagement potential (both for the choir during rehearsal, and for the audience) as well as the educational growth of the choir.

Entertainment / Engagement Potential

This, of course, again depends on the people in your context to a large extent. When planning a concert, you could choose one major well-known piece(s) by a composer (like Handel's *Messiah)*, or plan around a nation (like a concert of all French repertoire) or choose a theme (like war for a Remembrance Day Concert).

I have usually tried to choose music that had a lot of variation to keep the interest of both the choir and future audience (so, for example, one concert included Mozart, Vivaldi, a South African freedom song, a psalm setting, a Billy Joel tune and *Spider Pig* from *The Simpsons Movie*). Because the goal of the community choirs I have worked with was gentle evangelism, I have always tried to include both secular and sacred music. Many great secular composers still deal with the big themes of love, life, death (you know—life, the universe and everything) that allows opportunities for discussion about how that connects to God.

For example, I would argue performing *Amazing Grace* or any African-American spiritual without prayerfully exploring the meaning of the text would be missing the whole point of the piece. The context it was written in and the people who wrote it; the fact that John Newton (composer of *Amazing Grace*) used to be a slave trader before he was converted; the evils of slavery; the church's historic part in the slave trade; and the continued systemic racist structures in our society are all essential to understanding the music. To perform this piece properly is to sing not only of God's love and amazing grace, but to lament both our racist present and past.

Educational Growth of the Choir

Additionally, I always wanted the choirs I worked with to grow and develop. Even if people only joined for fun, a chance to meet people and for a community they could belong to, they still wanted to improve.

From my perspective, their folder should always hold:

- Some music that they find very easy
- Some music that fits in their comfort zone, with a little challenge
- Some music that is more challenging and creates growth
- One piece from a previous year that they loved, to go to even deeper musical depths
- One piece of music that is an extreme challenge for them that we would work on for the whole year.

For the Very First Rehearsal of the Choir

I would always start with a round—something like *Dona Nobis Pacem* or the Congolese folk song *Banaha* (incidentally, these make great pieces to start a concert with…the choir at the back and gradually adding in voices as they slowly walk through the congregation / audience to the front). The round gives the choir a chance to learn everything together in one simple unison line, but easily expands to sound richer and more complex once secure. Both examples above can be done as a round in two parts or in three parts.

For the very first rehearsal, I would also prepare a couple of two-part pieces[15] as well as a couple of three-part pieces.[16] If there are enough strong people and a semi-decent balance, there is the possibility to move to four-part SATB pieces later.[17]

Lead Up to Performances

As we get closer to singing publicly, I always recommend moving from musical detail to the more emotive aspects of the piece; does the choir understand and are they expressing the emotional content of the words (especially if singing in a different language)? No matter how technically perfect the music may be (or not), that is only the starting point—the music is between the notes. Even if there are a lot of technical issues and parts that are insecure, the audience will remember the performance that made them feel something, instead of the one that was technically flawless.

Additionally, I recommend focusing more and more on the positive, and reinforcing the confidence of the choir. Lastly, if there is still detailed work to be done (and there nearly always is), I recommend rehearsing those difficult sections quickly in short bursts and spend most of the time running larger sections of the piece so that the choir understands how everything fits together as a whole.

Analyzing the Church's Experience—Case Studies

5

> Music does not simply communicate doctrinal truths in a way that reinforces memory of them, as if it affected only the mental faculties; nor does music simply appeal to the senses, which would lead to an insistence that they here rise above the aural appeal. Rather, music combines the emotional power of sound with the spiritual power of God's Word in such a way as to affect the sound.[18]

Having explored the practical, organizational and musical steps to starting a community choir, let us examine a few examples of how using a community choir has been approached missionally in different contexts. While there are understandably similarities between the case studies, it is important to note that aspects of their differing approaches might not be applicable or appropriate for your context at this time. Adapt as you see fit. We will briefly explore four different case studies.

St Michael's Teen Worship Band (Calgary, Canada)

I was hired as a part-time music minister to focus on organizing various musical teams and leading worship from the drum kit for the teen service at this church. Out of the four services every weekend, the teen service had the lowest numbers in attendance (about 250 on average) and there was a full-time music minister who led worship at the three other services.

There was a three-fold intent behind the Teen Band. The first followed the example of Hillsong establishing Hillsong United. We recognized that while the current worship band was strong in terms of quality (it consistently had excellent professional musicians with a deep faith leading worship), we were at least a generation away from the teens we were trying to reach. The age gap and difference in musical tastes was increasingly noticeable. Secondly, there was a desire to build up young musicians, give coaching about the practicalities of performing live and leading worship, and give them the opportunity to lead worship in front of their peers. And lastly, the goal was to have a small team of instrumentalists that could back an ever-increasing number of vocalists. Although I never called it a choir (they thought it sounded cooler to say they were in a band), and although there were only 7 singers when I was called to a different ministry, the intention was gradually to increase the number of vocalists to form a choir.

We always started and ended any rehearsals with prayer or Scripture as well as praying for each other. The Teen Band only led worship at teen nights and was therefore part of a larger structure of worship, Scripture and teaching that the youth worker led—often having teens ministering to teens in a way that I would have been unable to do. I know that many teens met Christ through the music in that church community. And although I cannot give exact statistics, we had a large youth group that was blessed to have many annual baptisms and confirmations.

St Peter's, Belsize Park (London) and St Mary Magdalen, Chapelfields (Coventry)

Because I had experience of founding a new choir in Calgary, Canada with a group called *Cum Vino Cantus*, one of the first things I did as pastoral assistant at St Peter's and later as curate at St Mary Magdalen was to start a choir as both a form of outreach into the community and as a form of gentle evangelism.

With both choirs, we were keen to invite everyone regardless of faith or of no faith, with a mission statement that the choir 'first and foremost values the playful and relaxed pursuit of choral excellence.' The choirs were both inclusive in every way, were fun and focused on reaching out into the wider parish. We were not only helping people individually in terms of physical and mental health, but also reducing social isolation, increasing social networks and involvement in the community.

More importantly, we formed our own community that not only supported each other but had a focus of social action and civic engagement through the local charities we supported. All money donated at concerts went to charities such as the Coventry Resource Centre for the Blind or Marie Curie. All concerts were held in the church, and most were joint events with other local choirs to build relationships in the community, to increase the amount donated to the chosen charity and, to be blunt, to guarantee we had an audience for each other.

For both choirs, roughly a third of the members were Christian (only three or four joined from the church itself), there were a few of other faith backgrounds, some of no faith background, and a few quite strongly atheist. There were, as expected, many individual questions about Christianity and prayer requests as well as sharing of my faith and vocational journey with people on a regular basis.

Both choirs participated in leading worship by singing during services throughout the year. Some joined other social groups in the church, some started serving in other ministries like our dementia-friendly service and café, a couple started attending church again after years away and one woman shared that, because of her time in the choir, she was able to come back into a church building again after being abused by a vicar in the past. Many seeds were sown.

St Martin-in-the-Fields, Finham (Coventry)

I am grateful that the Rev'd Matt Taylor and his wife Sandra (a professional vocalist who directs the choir) were kind enough to talk to me about the gospel choir at St Martin's. The choir at St Martin's was started with just a few church members and gradually brought in outside community members. As it grew, there was still a nucleus of church members, but a community focus on well-being and mental health of those involved developed.

They are unashamedly Christian throughout everything they do, sometimes starting with prayer and always being available for individual prayer if requested. The musical choices are consistently gospel or praise and worship music, and the choir sometimes performs in services, as well as at other church events. Because of that, the members feel a strong sense of belonging and are part of the church family.

As a vehicle for mission, there is a sense of gentle evangelism that Matt Taylor said 'brings in people to services, but more importantly, also engages with those on the outskirts of the church.' Sandra mentioned that 'There is a lot of laughter and joy...people come along with their aches and pains of the day. During the rehearsal they relax and have fun, then go home uplifted. If they can associate that with church, that's great.'

Three of the original members died during the COVID-19 pandemic and the choir were asked to sing at one of the memorial services. Sandra stated, 'One of the moving moments of the choir has been seeing a person who has little or no faith singing *Ain't Nobody like Jesus*...or to see someone who is often alone and socially isolated singing *I am Not Alone* with the choir and recognizing they are actually not alone is powerful. This gospel choir is part of people's faith journey. It will allow them to be changed.'

St John the Divine, Willenhall (Coventry)

I am grateful that the Rev'd Charlotte Jackson, curate at St John the Divine, was willing to talk with me about the community choir started by the vicar, the Rev'd Pam Howell, out of Willenhall parish church. It was originally set up as a church outreach ministry through funding from a Good Neighbours Project for those who were 55+, with the aim to battle social isolation and loneliness by bringing people together who otherwise do not get much social interaction or connection. Although it has not stayed exclusively 55+, it is still aimed at that age bracket.

As opposed to the other case studies, this choir uses only words and learns by rote, often singing along to recorded YouTube or karaoke tracks. They sing a mixture of secular and sacred music—including a lot of pop songs or musicals—with their repertoire, often suggested by the members of the choir themselves, and have built up a large selection of pieces they enjoy singing.

The vicar and members of the group regularly pray for each other and rehearsals often open with prayer. Several members have started attending other social events and ministries, such as the Women's Fellowship. Additionally, a lot of thought is put into organizing car sharing and rides for each other to ensure no one is left out. The choir regularly sings in church, leads Carols in the Pub at a local pub, and are often asked to sing for community events, where children have started coming out of the audience and singing along with the choir. Jackson stated that, 'The community choir is embedded in the wider church community. They belong to and feel a part of the church. It is a matter of belonging before you believe.'

6

Conclusion

> Let the word of Christ dwell in you richly…and with gratitude in your hearts sing psalms, hymns, and spiritual songs to God. (Col 3.16)

In this brief booklet, we have attempted to explore some scriptural, theological and practical ideas for using a community choir as an evangelistic outreach tool gently to bring people to Christ. I hope it has given you a place to start thinking about how you might be able to form a community choir to support those of your parish or neighbourhood…and with gratitude in your hearts sing psalms, hymns and spiritual songs to God!

Notes

1 D Cartlidge and J Elliott, *Art and the Christian Apocrypha* (London: Routledge, 2001) p 15.
2 D Engh, 'Why Use Music in English Language Learning? A Survey of the Literature' in *English Language Teaching* (Vol 6, No 2, 2013, doi:10.5539/elt.v6n2p113) pp 113–127.
3 A Milbank, 'Apologetics in the Imagination: Making Strange' in A Davison (ed), *Imaginative Apologetics: Theology, Philosophy and the Catholic Tradition* (London: SCM Press Ltd, 2011) p 32.
4 A Davison (ed), *Imaginative Apologetics: Theology, Philosophy and the Catholic Tradition* (London: SCM Press, 2011) p 31.
5 K Rahner, 'Theology and the Arts' in G Thiessen (ed), *Theological Aesthetics* (London: SCM Press, 2004) p 219.
6 M O'Connor, 'The Singing of Jesus' in J Begbie and S Gunthrie (eds), *Resonant Witness: Conversations Between Music and Theology* (Grand Rapids, MI: William B Eerdmans, 2011) pp 434–435.
7 M Luther, 'Preface to Georg Rhau's *Symphoniae iucundae*' in G Thiessen (ed), *Theological Aesthetics* (London: SCM Press, 2004) p 145.
8 Rookmaaker quoted in G Cray, 'Through Popular Music: "Wholly Holy?"' in J Begbie, *Beholding the Glory: Incarnation Through the Arts* (Grand Rapids, MI: Baker Book House, 2001) pp 135–136.
9 M Charles-Murray, 'The Emergence of Christian Art,' in G Spier (ed), *Picturing the Bible: The Earliest Christian Art* (London: Yale University Press, 2007) p 61.
10 R Jensen, 'Early Christian Images and Exegesis,' in G Spier (ed), *Picturing the Bible: The Earliest Christian Art* (London: Yale University Press, 2007) p 84.
11 *ibid*, p 84.
12 W Dyrness, *Poetic Theology: God and the Poetics of Everyday Life* (Grand Rapids, MI: Eerdmans Publishing Company, 2011) p 151.
13 Linguistically, a diphthong is a sound created by the combination of two vowels. Sometimes that is intended like the word 'coin' or 'joy,' where the sound begins in the first vowel and then glides into the second vowel. We need to be conscious of doing that together as singers, leaning into the first open vowel and not allowing the second vowel to constrict the voice. There is also the danger of creating extra diphthong vowel sounds when they are not intended, which often happens when singing in Latin (a language without diphthongs).
14 Both solfa and solfège refer to a system of using syllables like 'do, re, mi, fa, so' to teach sight-singing. (Think of Julie Andrews singing *Do-Re-Mi* in *The Sound of Music*.)
15 Usually, one high voice part and one low voice part that can be split to match vocal ranges across gender.
16 Usually, SAB = Soprano (high female), Alto (low female), and Baritone (male).
17 SATB = Soprano (high female), Alto (low female), Tenor (high male), Bass (low male).
18 J Irwin, '"So Faith Comes from What Is Heard": The Relationship between Music and God's Word in the First Two Centuries of German Lutheranism' in J Begbie and S Gunthrie (eds), *Resonant Witness: Conversations Between Music and Theology* (Grand Rapids, MI: William B Eerdmans Publishing Co, 2011) p 71.